WOOD CRAFT LOVE

Vintage-Inspired Home Décor Projects You Can Make

Design Originals

an Imprint of Fox Chapel Publishing

www.d-originals.com

CONTENTS

PROJECTS

INTRODUCTION

This book will inspire you to turn ordinary craft wood pieces into stunning home décor with 17 project ideas that would make any interior designer swoon. All you have to do is combine ready-made pieces found at craft and hobby stores with unique items you find at flea markets, garage sales, and thrift stores, and then dress them up with creative paint finishes to make one-of-a-kind masterpieces. You'll find ideas for furniture, wall art, fixtures, and more in this book, and you'll only need a few simple tools, paints, and your creativity to make them—no special woodworking skills required! Plus, we'll review the best techniques for using chalk-finish paints, waxes, spray paints, decoupage, and stencils, plus tips for acquiring those secondhand treasures at a bargain.

I've made it my business and my ultimate pleasure to find and turn items from yard sales, thrift stores,

craft stores, and auctions into amazing furnishings and accessories. I love the thrill of finding a piece and repurposing it while keeping the character of the old piece alive through its transformation. I've also trained my eye for mixing old and new and for using just the right finish, making pieces look like heirlooms or high-end furniture. These are things you can learn to do, too!

Upcycling means taking something used or discarded and turning it in to a new piece that is more useful, and often more beautiful, than the original. The concept of upcycling has been around for generations—during the difficult economic times of the 1930s and 1940s, families repurposed items over and over to get the most use out of them. Although being thrifty and upcycling are trendy today because of their positive impact on the environment, there are those—like me!—who upcycle for the artistic

value as well as the economic savings. Finding an old lamp in your basement and envisioning it as table base, or buying a pair of porcelain vases at a garage sale and creating chic bookends out of them, are both ways to add personal style to your home without spending a lot of money. I've also discovered that the paths of upcycling and crafting often cross, as paint, fabric, and other finishing touches are used to transform an unused piece of junk into a beautiful, "Where did you get that?!" treasure.

You can find inspiration for your work in a lot of places. Immerse yourself in magazines, websites, and blogs dedicated to photos of charming spaces. That will inspire and motivate you. Personally, Pinterest has been my biggest source of creative inspiration. I find myself there daily over my morning cup of coffee. You're also sure to be inspired while shopping for upcyclables. Sometimes certain items just really catch your eye. If you are shopping at local sales, be sure to arrive early, smile, carry cash, and get the item you like! If it's a unique item that you have your eye on, it won't be there for long. Do your best to develop a relationship with people whose shops and markets you visit often, because you'll find that they will graciously look out for you when you visit them.

The fact is that it can sometimes take time to acquire all the things you need for an upcycling project. But you will find the materials you're dreaming of! It's the creative process—enjoy it and know that the end result will be beautiful.

A designer and decorator for 15 years, Jodie Landry runs a boutique, Pieces, in York, Pennsylvania, where she sells her unique vintage-inspired, upcycled items. The married mother of three teenage boys has also outfitted her home with many of her fabulous finds that mix in perfectly with her self-described "comfortable with just a touch of bling" style. She loves what she does, and says that her journey of making things pretty and finding unique uses for items has been nothing short of amazing.

Jodie Landry

GETTING STARTED: JUST ADD PAINT

All you need to get started is something to paint and something to paint it with!

Crafting something out of wood usually requires an array of tools, woodworking knowledge, and a large work space, but don't worry! Pre-cut wood items in basswood, pine, and Baltic birch are available in craft stores everywhere, eliminating the need to create the items yourself. These ready-made products come in a variety of sizes and shapes. Most are already sanded, so you can work on them in your home without the need for a workshop. Wood items previously sold mainly to carvers and wood burners are finding new life as home décor pieces for crafters like you. They are just begging to be enhanced with creative finishes and embellishments and made a part of your home.

Before you start painting your pieces, it is best to figure out the end result you are after. Take a look at the finishing techniques shown on pages 8–11 and select the one that will give your project the appearance you are going for. Don't worry if you're not quite satisfied with the initial results—one nice feature of chalk-finish paint and spray paint, two of the finish options explored in this book, is that they are easy to paint over. If you're not happy with your first color choice, you can always go back and change it. Read the tips on the following pages, don't sweat the small stuff, and have fun!

Chalk-finish paint and other finishes make wood blanks into beautiful custom creations full of personality.

Wood blanks are available in dozens of sizes, shapes, and styles for all your crafting needs.

A GUIDE TO FINISHES

There are many kinds of finishes that you can use for the projects in this book and for your own creations. Take a look at these tips and techniques for a variety of finishes before getting started, and you'll be equipped for any project you tackle!

Chalk-Finish Paint

Chalk-finish paint is growing in popularity as one of the best paints to use on furniture and other home décor items because of its versatility. It's easy to use and manipulate, requires no sanding or priming of the surface to be painted, will adhere to almost any surface, and produces a time-worn finish that is coveted by interior designers.

The natural finish of this paint is matte (chalky), but you can buff it to get a satin-type luster. One coat is all that is needed on most surfaces, depending on the color you use. Furniture wax or varnish is recommended to protect and seal the surface after painting. To keep the finish looking fresh, waxes should be reapplied every six to twelve months, depending on how often the piece is used or handled.

There are many brands of chalk-finish paint on the market, but you can also make your own. An abundance of recipes can be found online, using everything from gypsum plaster (plaster of Paris) and non-sanded grout to calcium carbonate mixed into a flat latex paint. Each ingredient has pros and cons to its use, so be sure to research thoroughly.

Distressing

Using either water or sandpaper, it's easy to give chalk-finish paint a distressed look. The water method uses a soft, damp rag to wipe recently applied paint off of a piece. It works best on pieces where the paint has been applied over an existing layer of finish or chalk-finish paint. Use this technique within 15-45 minutes of paint application.

The sandpaper method, used once the paint has dried, gives you more control. Use fine-grit sandpaper and a light touch for a slightly distressed look or large-grit sandpaper to remove more paint for a rustic look. You can sand either before or after waxing, just be sure to reapply wax over any unsealed areas.

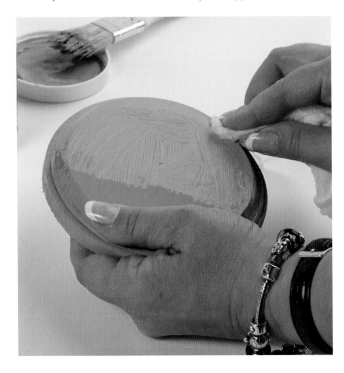

Layering Colors

A piece of furniture that shows its history through layers of exposed paint colors can be beautiful. You can mimic this look easily by layering chalk-finish paint. Apply a basecoat and let it dry. Then rub a hard wax, like a candle or paraffin bar, over the areas where you want the base color to show through. This is called a resist technique, as the wax will resist any layers of paint you apply on top of it, protecting the base color so it can be exposed later. Wipe away any excess wax and apply a contrasting color of paint over the entire piece. Once dry, use sandpaper to remove the topcoat from the resist areas (those covered with the wax). Be sure to finish the project with a wax or varnish to seal it.

Dry Brushing

Using a dry brush technique with chalk-finish paint is a simple way to create a weathered look. After applying your basecoat and letting it dry, put a small amount of a contrasting color on a dry paintbrush. Use long, light strokes to apply the paint, reloading your brush as needed.

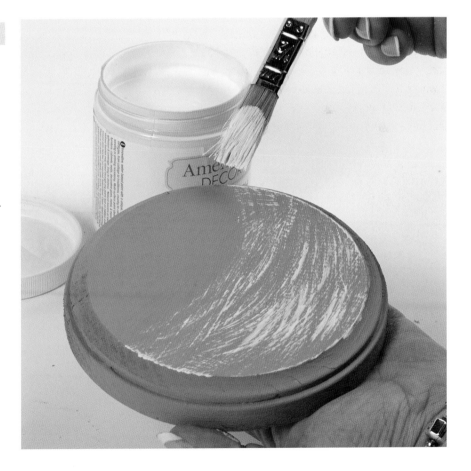

Crème Waxes

Crème waxes are available in clear varieties, as well as dark varieties, which can range from light gold to deep brown. When applying a wax finish, there are a few important points to remember:

- Use a brush or lint-free rag to apply wax. Wipe off any excess immediately.
- Always use very thin, uniform coats. It is better to apply multiple thin coats than one thick layer. Be sure to let the wax dry completely before applying another coat.
- Do not apply wax to pieces that will be used outdoors.
- When using a dark wax, always test it on a small area of your project first, as it can change the intensity of the piece's color (see tip below).
- If you are going to buff, use a clean, light-colored cloth; a dark cloth may discolor the finish.

Tip

It is best to apply a dark wax over a clear wax while it is still fresh; dark wax applied directly to a project's surface will discolor the paint and won't be as workable.

Chalkboard Paint

Not to be confused with chalk-finish paint, chalkboard paint can turn a wide range of surfaces into a chalkboard. This paint comes in spray-on and brush-on varieties. Chalkboard paint is available in traditional black, as well as numerous fun colors.

Stencils

Stencils can be used on any surface and come in a variety of sizes and designs. They are easy to use and do not require any artistic ability. Stencils can add dimension and personal flair to any project. Here are some points to help you perfect your stenciling technique:

- Tape the stencil to your project along the top and bottom edges to keep it in place.
- Use a foam dauber, small brush, or sponge to apply the paint.
- For best results, apply small amounts of paint in quick, up-and-down strokes.
- Start painting on the edges of the stencil and work your way toward the center. This helps prevent bleeding.
- Apply two thin coats rather than one thick coat. Don't remove the stencil until you are sure you are finished.
- If using acetate stencils, wash them regularly in warm water and store them flat to keep them in good condition.

Spray Paint

Spray paint has come a long way during the past few years. It can be used on many different surfaces, such as fabric, wood, glass, and plastic, and now comes in a wide range of colors and finishes, including metallic. It also is available in textures like stone and hammered metal.

Here are some basic tips to remember when using spray paints:

- Always start with a clean, dry surface. Be sure to sand hard surfaces and use a primer for best adhesion.
- Avoid direct sunlight and hot, humid weather when painting.
- Use an even side-to-side motion for application, overlapping your spray pattern with each pass. Begin and finish each pass off the object.
- Use multiple thin coats instead of one thick coat.

TOOL KIT

To make the projects in this book, all you need are a few simple tools and some general know-how to use them.

Drill & Drill Bits

A power drill can be used to drill holes and act as a screwdriver. For drilling holes, you'll need a general-purpose twist bit or a spade bit (for creating large holes). To use the drill as a screwdriver, you'll need a Phillips head screwdriver attachment. When drilling a hole for a screw, use a bit that is about the diameter of the screw's body, but smaller than the diameter of its body plus the threads. Always make sure the bit is tight in the drill before starting.

Nail Gun & Nails

A nail gun can be used in place of a hammer, but If you don't have a nail gun or aren't comfortable using one, a hammer will work just fine. If using a nail gun, be sure to wear safety glasses and practice on scrap wood before you start your project. Both the amount of pressure and the amount of time the pressure is applied to the nail gun will affect how smoothly and evenly the nail goes into the surface. Keep the tip of the gun against the surface and apply pressure using your hands only. There will be a kickback when you fire the gun, so don't hold it against your stomach or chest. Pull and release the trigger quickly to prevent multiple nails from shooting, as this could jam the gun. When you're finished, each nail head should be flush against the surface.

Screwdriver

Two basic screwdrivers are needed for the projects in this book: a flat head and a Phillips head. Or you can use screwdriver bits with a power drill. Depending on the size of the screw you are using, you may need to drill a starter hole in your project before adding the screw. Attach the screw by turning the screwdriver clockwise (to the right), applying downward pressure on the handle as you turn. Make sure the screw stays straight as it enters the wood. Don't hold on to the screw or rest your hand next to it in case the screwdriver slips off the screw head as you work.

Saw

A few projects require a hand saw (or a circular saw will allow you to work even faster). Secure the piece you are cutting with clamps or a miter box. Mark the wood with a guideline, and then score it with a utility knife. Make a few backward strokes on the line with your saw until you have a shallow groove. Then begin sawing using long, smooth, back-and-forth strokes.

Wire Cutters

Choose wire cutters with a grip span of 2½" to 3½" (6.5 to 9cm) to prevent pinching your fingers. Make sure the cutting edges are sharp, and always cut at right angles. Pull on the cutters when applying pressure; don't push them away from you.

Sandpaper

You will need fine-grit sandpaper for preparing surfaces and distressing finished pieces. Scuff smooth or shiny surfaces with sandpaper before spray-painting for better paint adhesion. Always remember to sand in one direction and along the grain.

Adhesives

There are many good adhesives on the market. E6000® Permanent Craft Adhesive was used for the projects in this book. It can be found in crafting, hobby, and hardware stores and is formulated to work with an array of mediums from wood and metal, to fabric and glass. Substitute your favorite adhesive product as desired.

SHABBY CHIC BIRDHOUSE CHANDELIER

Add a touch of whimsy to an old light fixture by replacing the bulbs with miniature wood birdhouses. This charming chandelier looks great hanging indoors or outside.

MATERIALS

- Old light fixture
- Miniature wood birdhouses (one for each arm on the light fixture)
- Spray paint: silver metallic
- Chalk-finish paint: white
- Clear matte spray varnish
- Strong adhesive (E6000 was used for this project)
- Fine-grit sandpaper

Create It Yourself

STEP ONE: Lightly sand the light fixture with fine-grit sandpaper.

STEP TWO: Spray the entire light fixture with metallic spray paint and let it dry.

STEP THREE: Apply a coat of white chalk-finish paint over the entire fixture and let it dry.

STEP FOUR: Once the fixture is dry, use fine-grit sandpaper to distress areas along the edges so the metallic paint shows through the white paint.

STEP FIVE: Paint the birdhouses with the white chalk-finish paint and let them dry.

STEP SIX: Once dry, glue one birdhouse to the top of each arm in the light fixture. A strong adhesive like E6000 is recommended.

STEP SEVEN: Spray the entire chandelier with a clear matte varnish.

UPCYCLED GLAM SIDE TABLE

Add a little drama to any room with this fabulous side table. It will fit just about anywhere and can easily be moved when entertaining. Believe it or not, this table is made using an old lamp base found at a garage sale and a wood oval sign plaque from the craft store. It's an inexpensive upcycle with fabulous results!

MATERIALS

- Secondhand lamp or lamp base
- 12" x 20" (30.5 x 51cm) wood oval plaque
- Nickel satin-finish spray paint
- Clear spray varnish
- Strong adhesive (E6000 was used for this project)
- Wire cutters or sharp utility scissors
- Fine-grit sandpaper

Create It Yourself

STEP ONE: Unplug your lamp and remove the bulb, lampshade, and all the hardware. You will only need the lamp base for this project. Using wire cutters or sharp utility scissors, carefully cut any wires from the lamp base.

STEP TWO: Lightly sand the lamp base using fine-grit sand paper.

STEP THREE: Apply a smooth coat of strong adhesive (such as E6000) to the back of the wood plaque. Carefully attach the plaque to the top of the lamp base. Place a book or other weight on top of the plaque and let the glue dry.

STEP FOUR: Cover the entire table with a light coat of spray paint and let it dry. Add additional coats of spray paint as desired until you have an even, opaque coating.

STEP FIVE: Finish the table with a coat of clear spray varnish.

The thrill of the hunt: Shopping at thrift stores and flea markets

- Know your style.
- Keep an open mind—old fabrics and ugly paint can easily be fixed.
- Shop early and shop often—the good stuff goes fast!
- Look for classic designs with "good bones."
- Look beyond the decorative furnishings—vintage glassware and linens hold lots of possibilities.
- Shop for seasonal items year round.

RUSTIC CHIC PALLET WALL SCONCE

Rustic meets elegant with this fabulous sconce that pairs a wood pallet with an upcycled candle sconce. A coat of spray paint over the entire piece ties the design together, making it a unique statement for any wall.

MATERIALS

- 24" x 12" (61 x 30.5cm) rustic pallet
- Secondhand candle sconce
- Chalk-finish paint: white and gray
- Spray paint: silver metallic
- Clear spray varnish
- Screwdriver or drill and 1 screw
- Fine-grit sandpaper

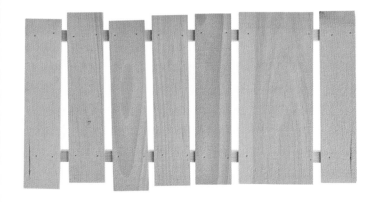

Create It Yourself

STEP ONE: Paint the pallet with white chalk-finish paint and let it dry.

STEP TWO: Spray-paint the candle sconce silver. Once dry, apply a coat of gray chalk-finish paint.

STEP THREE: Once dry, lightly sand the candle sconce with fine-grit sandpaper to expose some of the silver spray paint under the gray chalk-finish paint.

STEP FOUR: Center the screw on the pallet and attach it. Hang the candle sconce from the screw (depending on the sconce fixture, you may need to use a nail or adhesive instead).

STEP FIVE: Spray the entire piece with a varnish. You can use a matte or gloss varnish depending on the end look you want to achieve.

CHARMING COLLECTION SHELVES WITH RIBBON FINISH

If you are a collector and love to group and display your treasures, this simply designed shelf will give you added space in no time!

Create It Yourself

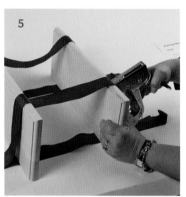

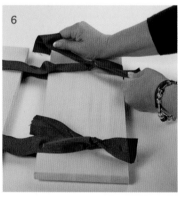

MATERIALS

- 12" x 16" (30.5 x 40.5cm) rectangular wood signboard
- 3 yd. (3m) of 1" (2.5cm)-wide grosgrain ribbon
- Paint or stain of your choice (optional)
- Saw
- Staple gun and staples
- Fine-grit sandpaper

STEP ONE: Measure the wood signboard and cut it in half so you have two 12" x 8" (30.5 x 20.5cm) pieces. Sand any raw edges of the wood pieces smooth. Paint or stain the shelves, or leave them unfinished.

STEP TWO: Cut two 64" (162.5cm)-long pieces of the ribbon, and then fold them in half. Cut a third 10" (25.5cm)-long piece and set it aside.

STEP THREE: Lay the two long ribbon pieces side by side with the folds at the top. Place a shelf between the tails of the left ribbon, about 16" (40.5cm) from the fold. Position the tails about 1" (2.5cm) in from the short left end of the shelf.

STEP FOUR: Staple the ribbon tails to the underside of the shelf, about ¼" (0.5cm) from the edge. Repeat on the right side of the shelf with the second ribbon.

STEP FIVE: Place the second shelf between the ribbon tails, about 10" (25.5cm) below the first shelf. Position the ribbon tails as before and staple them in place.

STEP SIX: Knot the loose ribbon tails tightly together in pairs under the second shelf. You can let any extra ribbon hang down as a decoration or cut it off.

STEP SEVEN: Take the 10" (25.5cm) piece of ribbon you cut earlier and feed it through the ribbon loops at the top of the shelves. Tie the 10" (25.5cm) ribbon in a knot, pulling the two ribbon loops together over the center of the top shelf.

FRENCH BISTRO WALL RACK

Need a handy place to hang your keys, the dog's leash, or your favorite hat? This little rack can take on a personality all its own depending on the type of pulls or hooks you decide to put on it. If using chalkboard paint, leave room at the top so you can write yourself reminders as you head out the door.

Create It Yourself

STEP ONE: Paint the signboard with black chalkboard paint and let it dry.

STEP TWO: Use a strong adhesive (such as E6000) to mount your pulls/hooks to the board. Check the manufacturer's instructions for use and drying time, and give the adhesive plenty of time to cure before you attempt hanging anything on the pulls or hooks.

STEP THREE: Attach a picture hanger to the back of the rack for mounting on the wall.

MATERIALS

- Paneled wood signboard
- Secondhand pulls and/or hooks (or purchase from hardware store)
- Picture hanger with necessary tools for attaching
- Chalkboard paint: black
- Strong adhesive (E6000 was used for this project)

VINTAGE-INSPIRED BOOKENDS

This idea is so easy and fun you'll be making bookends for every shelf in your home!
You can use vases, figurines, toys, or just about any solid object that can be painted.
Try some of the different finishing techniques from the Start with the Finish section
and see what you come up with!

MATERIALS

- 2 small carving blocks or 1 large block cut in half
- Secondhand vases (or any solid object of your choice)
- Chalk-finish paint: gray and white
- Clear matte spray varnish
- Strong adhesive (E6000 was used for this project)
- Saw (optional)

Create It Yourself

STEP ONE: Carving blocks come in a multitude of sizes. Cut a large one in half or use two smaller blocks for this project.

STEP TWO: Use a strong adhesive (such as E6000) to glue your chosen objects to the top of each wood block and let them dry.

STEP THREE: Coat both bookends with spray paint or chalk-finish paint. The vases in this piece were layer-painted with gray and white chalk-finish paint.

STEP FOUR: Finish both bookends with a clear matte spray varnish.

FRENCH PROVINCIAL STOOL

Make this sweet little stool with a touch of Parisian flair by mixing a craft wood signboard with legs from the hardware/lumber store. The distressed paint finish and stencil design give it an heirloom appeal that makes it truly gift worthy—if you can stand to part with it!

MATERIALS

- 12" x 20" (30.5 x 51cm) French Provincial signboard
- 4 wood legs from hardware/lumber store with pre-drilled holes
- Chalk-finish paint: gray and black
- Acrylic paint: silver metallic
- Stencil
- Drill and bits
- Screwdriver or drill and 4 screws
- Fine-grit sandpaper

Create It Yourself

STEP ONE: Measure and mark the back of the signboard with the location of the legs.

STEP TWO: Drill four holes through the signboard for the screws. Then use the screws to attach the legs to the signboard.

STEP THREE: Paint the entire piece with gray chalk-finish paint and let it dry.

STEP FOUR: Using black paint, add a stencil design to the top of the stool using the technique outlined on page 11.

STEP FIVE: Once the stencil paint is dry, use the sandpaper to lightly distress the top and legs of the stool, including the stenciled area, to give it a timeworn look.

STEP SIX: Brush a light coat of silver metallic paint onto the legs and around the edge of the signboard.

EVERY OCCASION CHALKY BANNERS

Create these versatile banners that can convey any sentiment for any occasion via a chalkboard paint finish. Precut banner shapes with holes for stringing can be found at most large craft stores. All you need to do is add paint and some ribbon or twine and you're all set to party!

Create It Yourself

STEP ONE: Paint all of the small wood tags with black chalkboard spray paint and let them dry.

STEP TWO: Make your own burlap banner shapes following the instructions below, or purchase premade shapes that you can string onto your twine.

STEP THREE: Glue a wood tag to the center of each burlap banner piece and let everything dry. Then string each burlap piece onto the twine.

STEP FOUR: Tie thin fabric strips onto the twine between each of the burlap pieces.

Making Your Own Burlap Banner Pieces

STEP ONE: Cut 12" (30.5cm)-long pieces of 3½" (9cm) burlap ribbon. Cut the same number of burlap pieces as the number of wood tags you have.

STEP TWO: Fold each piece of burlap in half widthwise, bringing the short ends together. Press each fold with your hands to crease it.

STEP THREE: Open the burlap pieces and apply adhesive across the width of each one about ½" (1.5cm) from the fold. It is important to leave this space between the fold and the glue line so the pieces can be strung onto your twine. Refold the pieces and let them dry.

STEP FOUR: Cut a triangular notch out of the bottom (non-folded) edge of each burlap piece to give it a banner shape.

MATERIALS

- Wood tags (number will depend on your desired banner message)
- Burlap ribbon or precut burlap banner pieces to match number of wood tags
- Twine
- Fabric strips
- Chalkboard spray paint: black
- Adhesive (E6000 was used for this project)

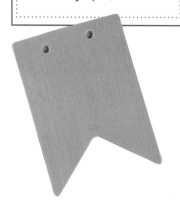

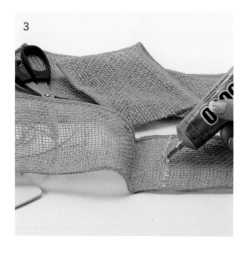

PHOTO TRANSFER TRAY

Why use standard frames for displaying photos in your home? With the photo transfer mediums available at craft stores, you can now put photos on just about anything! Use this piece as a tray, or give it a twist by making it a unique wall hanging.

MATERIALS

- 11" x 15" (28 x 38cm) wood serving tray
- Photo of your choice
- Decorative nail heads
- Chalkboard paint: black
- Chalk-finish paint: white (optional)
- Photo transfer medium
- Matte decoupage medium (like Mod Podge) or finishing spray

Create It Yourself

STEP ONE: Paint the sides of the tray with black chalkboard paint. You can also paint the bottom of the tray with black, just make sure you leave the area where you will place your photo unpainted, or paint it white. Let everything dry.

STEP TWO: Make a photocopy of the image you want to transfer onto printer paper—don't use a real photo or one printed from an inkjet printer. Keep in mind that the transfer method will produce a mirror image of your photo. Mirror the image on the photocopier or your computer if you prefer the look of the original. Both color and black and white photos will transfer well.

STEP THREE: Once your tray is dry, apply a thick layer of the transfer medium to the photocopy and place it face down on the tray, smoothing out any bubbles or creases. Let this dry for 24 hours. Once dry, use a damp cloth or sponge to wet one section of the paper at a time. Begin to rub gently to remove the paper and expose the image.

Repeat until all the paper has been removed. Note: Be sure to consult the manufacturer's instructions for your transfer medium, as it might work differently.

STEP FOUR: Apply a layer of matte decoupage medium (such as Mod Podge) or a finishing spray over the transferred image to seal and protect it.

STEP FIVE: Hammer the nail heads around the edge of the tray for a decorative finish.

CHORE CHART

Keeping track of the household chores never looked so good! This beauty will keep your family organized and your home neat and tidy, all while doubling as a piece of wall art.

MATERIALS

- 10" x 36" (25.5 x 91.5cm) flat wood board
- 12" x 20" (30.5 x 51cm) French Provincial signboard
- 7 small satin silver binder clips
- 2 miniature chipboard clipboards
- Paper of your choice
- Chalk-finish paint: black and white
- Clear crème wax
- Adhesive (E6000 was used for this project)
- Screwdriver or drill and 9 screws

Tip

For easy lettering in Step 2, use a paint pen or marker.

Create It Yourself

STEP ONE: Search your garage, flea markets, or lumber store for a large flat board. This piece was made using an old dining table leaf. Paint it with black chalk-finish paint and let it dry.

STEP TWO: Paint the signboard with white chalk-finish paint. When dry, paint something fun like "Work for Hire" or "Smith Family Chores" on the signboard.

STEP THREE: When the lettering is dry, apply a clear crème wax to both boards to seal the paint.

STEP FOUR: Along the bottom of the signboard, measure and mark the locations for seven screws that will hold the binder clips. Then attach the screws.

STEP FIVE: Use a strong adhesive (such as E6000) to glue the signboard onto the large black board.

STEP SIX: Attach the remaining screws to the black board, next to the signboard. Use these to hang additional items on the chart like miniature clipboards.

STEP SEVEN: Add the paper of your choice to the clipboards and binder clips.

NATURAL WOOD ENTERTAINING SET

Bring the outdoors in with this rustic-chic dessert stand and menu board! These projects can be whipped up quickly before your next party.

MATERIALS

- Extra-large bark edge round plaque
- Small bark edge round plaque
- Extra-large bark edge oval plaque
- Secondhand candlestick
- Secondhand wineglass
- Secondhand drawer pull (or purchase from hardware store)
- Chalk
- Chalkboard paint: black
- Strong adhesive (E6000 was used for this project)
- Screwdriver or drill and 1 screw (optional)

Create It Yourself

STEP ONE: For the dessert stand set, use a strong adhesive to attach the candlestick to the bottom of one of the round plaques. Repeat with the wineglass. Make sure the candlestick and glass are centered on the plaques for stability. These look beautiful left unfinished, or you can apply a coat of paint if you want a different look.

STEP TWO: For the menu board, paint one side of the oval plaque with black chalkboard paint. When the paint is dry, glue or screw the decorative draw pull onto the plaque, positioning it upside down. Use the pull to hold your chalk.

HANDSOME PET BED

Pamper your pet with this cozy bed made out of a wood crate from the craft store. Your pet will feel like royalty in his personalized perch. This piece is so stylish, it will look great in any room of the house.

MATERIALS

- Large wood crate to fit your pet
- Fence toppers from hardware/lumber store
- Chalk-finish paint: gray, white, and black
- Clear crème wax
- Stencil
- Saw (optional)
- Nail gun and nails
- Fine-grit sandpaper

Create It Yourself

STEP ONE: Pull or saw off all but the bottom slat on one of the long sides of the crate.

STEP TWO: Paint the crate and fence toppers with gray chalk-finish paint and let them dry. Then add a layer of white chalk-finish paint on top of the gray. When everything has dried, use sandpaper to distress the edges so some of the gray paint shows through the white.

STEP THREE: Stencil the name of your pet on the front of the crate (the bottom slat you left attached in Step 1) with black chalk-finish paint.

STEP FOUR: Nail the fence toppers to the bottom corners of the crate for legs. Apply a clear coat of crème wax over the entire piece to seal the paint.

STEP FIVE: Buy or make a pillow to fit into the bottom of the crate.

Ets. C. BAILLY

MULTI-PURPOSE DECORATIVE BOXES

Wood boxes come in a variety of shapes and sizes at the craft store, but you might also be lucky enough to find one at a garage sale or flea market. The uses for these boxes are many—like a jewelry box, ring keeper, recipe box, or charging station, just to name a few. You can finish the boxes off with decorative feet, stencils, and decoupage, or line them with fabric for an extra luxe look.

Create It Yourself

STEP ONE: Paint your box with a layer of chalk-finish paint. All of the boxes shown were painted with gray, white, or blue. Once the paint is dry, distress it with fine-grit sandpaper.

STEP TWO: For a charging station, drill a hole in the back of the box large enough to accommodate your device's cord. Drill multiple holes for more than one device if desired.

STEP THREE: For a ring keeper, fill the box with batting. Cover the batting with fabric and glue it in place. Cut small holes in the fabric and thread twine or ribbon through them to tie the rings in place.

MATERIALS

- Wood boxes from craft store or flea market finds of varying sizes
- Fabric, batting, and twine (for ring keeper)
- Chalk-finish paint: gray, white, and blue
- Craft glue
- Drill and bits (for charger station)
- Fine-grit sandpaper

STYLISH HURRICANES

These oversized candleholders look great grouped together or sitting alone. You can dress them up for the holidays with greens, fill them with flowers or potpourri, or have them double as decorative candy jars.

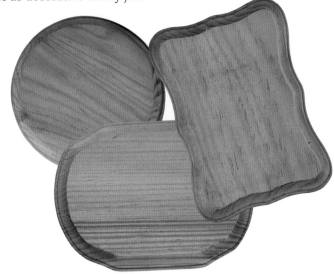

MATERIALS

- Secondhand wood or glass candlesticks
- Secondhand glass vases
- Small wood plaques (optional)
- Fabric strips (tassel) or ribbon
- Chalk-finish paint: black and gray
- Clear crème wax
- Adhesive (E6000 was used for this project)
- Fine-grit sandpaper

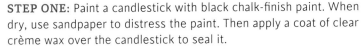

Create It Yourself

STEP ONE: Paint a candlestick with black chalk-finish paint. When dry, use sandpaper to distress the paint. Then apply a coat of clear crème wax over the candlestick to seal it.

STEP TWO: Use a strong adhesive to glue a glass vase on top of the candlestick. Tie ribbon or fabric strips around the base of the candlestick.

STEP THREE: You can also glue the candlestick to the bottom of a small wood plaque and then glue the glass vase on top of the plaque. The example shown at right was painted with a layer of black chalk-finish paint, then a layer of gray chalk-finish paint, and then distressed with sandpaper. A fabric strip tassel was added to the bottom.

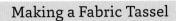

Making a Fabric Tassel

STEP ONE: Cut twenty to thirty 20" (50cm)-long strips of fabric. Set two strips aside.

STEP TWO: Gather the remaining strips together and fold them in half over one of the strip you set aside.

STEP THREE: Tie the remaining strip around the bundle about 1" (2.5cm) from the fold.

STEP FOUR: Use the piece the tassel is folded over to attach the tassel to the candle holder.

MOVEABLE STORAGE CRATE

Create your own stylish storage unit that's easy to move where you need it. It's much cooler than buying a boring shelf at your local home goods store, and you can orient and arrange the crates in the position you want.

MATERIALS

- 2 large wood crates
- 4 casters
- Chalk-finish paint: light blue and white
- Clear wax
- Adhesive (E6000 was used for this project)
- Nail gun and nails
- Screwdriver or drill and screws

Create It Yourself

STEP ONE: Use a strong adhesive (such as E6000) to glue the crates together. You can stack them vertically or horizontally depending on your needs. For extra stability, reinforce the connection by nailing the crates together after the glue has dried.

STEP TWO: Paint the crates with light blue chalk-finish paint and let them dry.

STEP THREE: Dry-brush a layer of white chalk-finish paint over the crates (see page 9). Once the paint has dried, seal the crates with a coat of clear wax.

STEP FOUR: Once the wax has dried, screw the casters onto the corners of the bottom crate.

How to drive a bargain

Here are some tips for negotiating a great price at a garage sale, flea market, or secondhand store.

- Pay attention to the seller while you are perusing the goods—is he flexible with others who are making offers?

- Ask the seller outright if prices are negotiable. If you are looking at a particular item, ask him the lowest price he will accept for it.

- Determine how much you are willing to pay for a particular item, and then offer this amount to the seller. Or, offer a lesser amount—the seller might take you up on your offer, and if he doesn't, you have room to negotiate up to the price you are willing to pay.

- Always be courteous and respectful toward the seller; never try to be intimidating. Friendliness will get you closer to your desired price.

LETTER ART

Typographic wall art is a great way to add a personal touch to your home. Wood letters come in all shapes and sizes so you can decorate your walls and shelves with names, monograms, or inspirational words. Have fun putting combinations together! Try different painting and finishing techniques, and see what creative ways you can come up with to make a statement.

MATERIALS

HOME SIGN

- 5" (12.5cm)-tall wood letters
- 6" x 24" (15 x 61cm) flat board
- Old book pages and music sheets
- 3 origami birds or other ornaments of your choice
- Natural twigs
- Twine
- Chalk-finish paint: white and light blue
- Matte decoupage medium
- Adhesive (E6000 was used for this project)
- Staple gun and staples
- Fine-grit sandpaper

LOVE SIGN

- 9" (23cm)-tall wood letters
- 10" x 44" (25.5 x 110cm) flat board
- Spray paint: oil-rubbed bronze
- Chalk-finish paint: light blue
- Adhesive (E6000 was used for this project)
- Hot glue gun and glue sticks
- Fine-grit sandpaper

"Home" Decoupage Sign

STEP ONE: Trace your chosen wood letters onto old book pages. Cut out the paper letters and use a matte decoupage medium to adhere them to their corresponding wood letters. Let everything dry.

STEP TWO: Once dry, apply decoupage medium over the letters to seal them.

STEP THREE: Paint the board with a layer of white chalk-finish paint and let it dry. Then add a layer of light blue chalk-finish paint. When dry, lightly distress the paint with sandpaper so some of the white paint shows through the blue.

STEP FOUR: Glue the letters onto the board in your desired configuration.

STEP FIVE: Use a staple gun to staple the twigs to the bottom edge of the board.

STEP SIX: Tie the origami birds, or any other ornament of your choice, to the twig with twine. Vary the lengths of twine used to tie on the ornaments so they hang down from the sign at different intervals.

"Love" Sign

STEP ONE: Use hot glue to create a pattern on the front of the wood letters and let it dry. Once dry, spray-paint the letters with bronze spray paint.

STEP TWO: Paint the board with light blue chalk-finish paint and let it dry. Once dry, lightly sand the paint to distress it.

STEP THREE: Use a strong adhesive to glue the letters onto the board in your desired configuration.

FABULOUS FRAMES

Craft wood frames come in all shapes and sizes, opening up the creative possibilities to enhance your home décor. Try painting frames of different styles in the same color palette to create an eye-catching gallery wall, or replace the glass with chicken wire or twine to make a custom jewelry display. Decorate a frame with plaster flowers and fill it with old sheet music instead of a photo for a unique piece of art. Let your imagination run wild!

Stenciled Frames

Three-Tier Ribbon Frames

STEP ONE: Paint several frames (the project shown uses three) of the same size with gray chalk-finish paint and let them dry.

STEP TWO: Using stencils, paint your chosen design onto each frame using white chalk-finish paint. Add details with a gold metallic pen if desired. If you have any small antique-looking frames, glue them into the picture opening in the middle of the wood frames to add some dimension.

STEP THREE: Cut 2½ yd. (2m) of ribbon. Fold it in half and tie a knot below to fold to form a loop.

STEP FOUR: Place the frames face down, spaced evenly apart. Place the ribbon on top of the frame backs and staple it in place with the staple gun.

Candlestick Frame

STEP ONE: Paint a square wood frame with gray chalk-finish paint and let it dry. Once dry, use your thumb, pinky, and index finger to paint spots on the frame with black chalk-finish paint. Varying the size of the spots by using different fingers will create an animal-type print. When the paint is dry, distress the frame with sandpaper.

STEP TWO: Color an ornamental cutout (the project shown uses a birdcage) with the silver paint pen. Glue the ornament to one of the bottom corners of the frame.

STEP THREE: Glue the bottom of the frame to the top of a candlestick (try to find one with a wax catcher).

STEP FOUR: Cut three 12" (30.5cm)-long strips of burlap, and tie them around the candlestick.

Union Jack Frame

STEP ONE: Select two frames, both with the same window size, one with outer dimensions about 1" (2.5cm) smaller than the other. The frames shown have a 4" x 6" (10 x 15cm) window size. Paint both frames with gray chalk-finish paint.

STEP TWO: Draw stripes on the large frame to mimic the Union Jack. Paint the center stripes and the areas between the stripes with black chalk-finish paint.

STEP THREE: Let the paint dry for 15 minutes, and then wet sand the painted areas between the stripes (see page 8).

STEP FOUR: Once the paint is completely dry, lightly distress the frame with sandpaper. Outline the stripes with a silver metallic paint pen.

STEP FIVE: Using a word stencil, add a word design to the small frame with black chalk-finish paint.

STEP SIX: Color the ornamental cutout (the project shown uses a chandelier) with the silver paint pen. Glue the cutout to one of the lower corners of the small frame.

STEP SEVEN: Glue the small frame on top of the large frame, aligning the windows.

MATERIALS

- Adhesive (E6000 was used for this project)
- Fine-grit sandpaper

Three-Tier Ribbon Frames

- Several wood frames of the same size
- Small antique-looking frames (optional)
- 2½ yd. (2.5m) of 1" (2.5cm)-wide ribbon
- Chalk-finish paint: white and gray
- Paint pen: gold metallic
- Stencils
- Staple gun and staples

Union Jack Frame

- Two wood frames with the same window size, one 1" (2.5cm) smaller than the other
- Wood ornamental cutout
- Chalk-finish paint: black and gray
- Paint pen: silver metallic
- Word stencil

Candlestick Frame

- Square wood frame
- Secondhand candlestick
- Wood ornamental cutout
- Three 12" x 1" (30.5 x 2.5cm) strips of burlap (or thin burlap ribbon)
- Chalk-finish paint: black and gray
- Paint pen: silver metallic

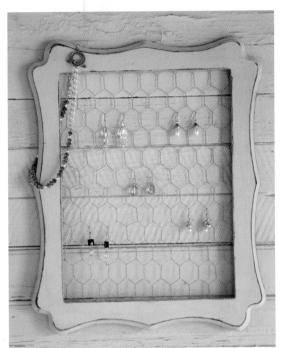

Chicken Wire Frame

STEP ONE: Paint an 11" x 14" (28 x 35cm) frame with black chalk-finish paint. When dry, add a layer of gray chalk-finish paint.

STEP TWO: Distress the edges of the frame with sandpaper, allowing some of the black paint to show through the gray.

STEP THREE: Cut a piece of chicken wire about 1" (2.5cm) larger on all sides than the frame's window. Staple the chicken wire in place on the back of the frame using a staple gun.

MATERIALS

CHICKEN WIRE FRAME

- 11" x 14" (28 x 35cm) wood frame
- Chicken wire
- Chalk-finish paint: black and gray
- Staple gun and staples
- Wire cutters

Plaster of Paris Flower Frame

STEP ONE: Mix gypsum plaster powder (plaster of Paris) with water at a ratio of 3 parts plaster to 1 part water. Dip the faux flowers into the wet plaster and allow them to dry and harden overnight.

STEP TWO: Paint an 8" x 10" (20 x 25cm) wood frame with gray chalk-finish paint. When the paint is dry, distress the frame with sandpaper. Spray the entire frame with a matte varnish.

STEP THREE: Using a strong adhesive, glue the flowers to the frame.

STEP FOUR: Fill the frame with old sheet music or an old book page.

MATERIALS

- 8" x 10" (20 x 25cm) wood frame
- Silk flowers
- Old sheet music or book pages
- Chalk-finish paint: gray
- Clear matte spray varnish
- Gypsum plaster (plaster of Paris)

THIRD
EYE
MEDITATIONS

THIRD
EYE
MEDITATIONS

Awaken Your
Mind, Spirit,
and Intuition

SUSAN SHUMSKY, DD

WEISER
BOOKS

This edition first published in 2020 by Weiser Books, an imprint of
Red Wheel/Weiser, LLC
With offices at:
65 Parker Street, Suite 7
Newburyport, MA 01950
www.redwheelweiser.com

ISBN: 978-1-57863-672-3

Library of Congress Cataloging-in-Publication Data available upon request.

Cover and interior design by Kasandra Cook
Typeset in Palatino

Printed in Canada
MAR

10 9 8 7 6 5 4 3 2 1

Disclaimer

Third Eye Meditations can introduce you to the complex field of meditation, visualization, affirmation, and mantra, but in no way claims to fully teach the techniques described. This book is not an independent guide for self-healing. Susan Shumsky is not a medical doctor and does not diagnose or cure diseases or prescribe treatments. No medical claims are implied about any methods in this book, even if specific "benefits" or "healing" of conditions are mentioned. Readers are advised to consult a medical doctor or psychiatrist before using any methods in this book. Susan Shumsky, her agents, assignees, licensees, and authorized representatives, as well as Divine Revelation, Teaching of Intuitional Metaphysics, and Weiser Books, make no claim or obligation and take no legal responsibility for the effectiveness, results, or benefits of reading this book, of using the methods described, or of contacting anyone listed in this book or at *www.divinerevelation.org*; deny all liability for any injuries or damages incurred; and are to be held harmless against any claim, liability, loss, or damage caused by or arising from following any suggestions made in this book, or from contacting anyone mentioned in this book or at *www.divinerevelation.org*.

From the Author

Meditation is not a path. It is a realization that you are already the goal. Meditation is not a practice. It is the end of practice. It is a do-nothing program whereby stillness dominates. How can you master meditation? Do nothing, nothing, and less than nothing.

Contents

PART THREE
ILLUMINATING THE PLANET

PART FOUR
ILLUMINATING SPIRITUAL ENLIGHTENMENT